Somebody Better Say Something

Brenda Matthews

EbonyEnergy Publishing
A Highest Good Publications Company
Chicago, Illinois

EbonyEnergy Publishing
A Highest Good Publications Company
Permissions Department
P.O. Box 43476
Chicago, Illinois 60643-0476

Any resemblance to any person, living or dead unless otherwise noted is purely coincidental. Any errors or omissions in the text or accuracy of the text are accidental. Considerable effort has been made by both the author and the publisher to ascertain accuracy and precision in any objective detail presented in these writings.

Library of Congress Cataloguing-in-Publication Data
Brenda Matthews
Somebody Better Say Something / by Brenda Matthews
p.   cm.
ISBN: 1-59825-012-4   ISBN13: 978-1-59825-012-1
1.   Title
Library of Congress Control Number: 2006935800

Cover Art, Design and Layout: Barron Steward
Editorial: Lynda Bruce

Printed in the United States of America
First Printing

EbonyEnergy Publishing
A Highest Good Publications Company
P.O. Box 43476
Chicago, Illinois 60643-0476
773-779-8129 Office   779-8139 Fax
www.ebonyenergybooks.com
www.ebonyenergypublishing.com
www.ebonyenergy.com

Dedication

This book is dedicated to Sister Monica Cahill and to Mrs. Verna Ruth Simpson.

Acknowledgements

There are so many who have supported my work through the years. Neither time nor space will permit me to name each of them. Just know that I am blessed to have so many of you in my life and your value is priceless. I can only name a few and this I must do. To my parents, Joe and Ida Matthews, thank you for all of your encouragement and unconditional love. To the Chicago Poetry Community, I love you all. Naima Dawson, thank you for all you have done and your continued support is always appreciated my SISTAH!!! To my Pastors, Ray and Adrienne Berryhill, I love you; where would I be without your support and teachings. You have literally turned my life around. To my entire family, your support and encouragement have kept me grounded. Cortez Green, you are the beat of my heart and the inspiration pushing me towards the finish line. God has put an amazing network of women in my life. Some of them spend time in prayer just for me, some call me and bless me, others shield me and protect me. These women have my back and assist me in whatever capacity needed. I am blessed to have this network and they are the women of Taproots Inc., Kimberly Dean, Ida Matthews, Vivicea Matthews, Margie Pruett, Tonnie Townsend, The Women of Evangel World Outreach Center, Verlee Jackson, Shirley Jackson, Doris Simpson, Dottie Eaton, Linda Berryhill, Alana Eaton and a host of others. To Sorrow, Moementum, Odyssey, O.D., Triple Blak, J. Ivy, Avery R. Young, Malik Yusef and all the other poets who have been with me since the beginning. It does not matter when I call, you always come and I love you for that. Ms. Dawn Mitchell, thank you for your continued support.

Patrick Milton, Jamie Boyce, Sheree Blakemore, Jeff Eaton, and Pastor Warren Smith, thank you. You blessed me more than you will ever know!!!! There are many more, but all of you know how much I love and appreciate all of you.

Peace and Blessings,

Mama Brenda

CONTENTS

Introduction

The purpose of this book is to bless the hearts of those who look for truth in times of trouble. This book is intended to make sad hearts glad and to lift up bowed down heads. I have spent my life over the past 15 years speaking into the lives of people. I want to see those who have fallen through the cracks run across the victory finish line. I have a passion for people and a big heart for youth. As I pursue my dreams, I hope one day to see our nation's inner-city youth reach their maximum potential. I will never give up on those who the world has written off. I believe in the words of Author Myles Munroe when he says, "YOU WILL NEVER CHANGE WHAT YOU'RE WILLLING TO TOLERATE." And as our youth proceed to the next level, they can no longer live mediocre lives. Somebody Better Say Something before it is too late.

—*Mama Brenda Matthews*

FREEDOM FIGHTING FANNIE

Sister Fannie Lou Hamer
Fighting for freedom
Working for justice

Revolution the solution
For this social pollution
We now live in

Beautiful black sister
Beaten
Bruised
Bullied
But she remembered
Blessed are ye when men shall revile
And persecute you

In her spirit she cried freedom
In her spirit she cried change
With her voice she sang
This little light of mine I'm gonna let it shine

Fannie Lou Hamer
Sister
Soldier
Sick and tired of being
Sick and tired

And after all she fought for
After all she prayed for
After all she risked her life for
After all she hoped for

BLACK PEOPLE STILL DON'T VOTE

11

HE'S STILL MY SON

From the moment he took his first breath
I loved him unconditionally
With ten fingers and ten toes
A face that would warm the heart of a lion
You're mine and mine alone
As I hold you close to my breast
I feel your heart as it beats close to mine
Your heart beats as that of a warrior
Ready to conquer all that was positive
And destroying anything that was negative
While watching you grow up
I imagined what life would be like for us
Sending you off to school
Deciding what to fix for lunch
Or discovering your many talents
It was us baby you and me against the world

As the years rapidly passed
I now look into the eyes of a young man
And every time his eyes meet mine they ask me
Hey Mama what happened
And no matter what happened
This child now a grown man
Still remains my gift

The world looked at the color of his skin
And damned him before he even tried
The 'hood took him from me
The 'homeboys' raised him for me
He was a king and the people were his subjects
Subjecting them to his hate
To his jealousy
Leaving no room for errors

Because whatever he wanted he took
This boy was a master at playing the game
He robbed
He stole
He'd kill a nigger without even thinking
He'd put a gun to your head and watch you die
He'd even sing a song

Die nigger die
Die nigger die

This was a heartless cruel low down nigger
Someone you would love to pistol whip publicly
And let him know I ain't taking this no more

This was the brother
You personally wanted to pull the trigger
And watch him die
Watch him take his last breath and scream
Die nigger
Die nigger die
And when he closed his eyes you felt free
You felt safe 'cuz he got what he deserved right
But it's a known fact that even the bad people of this world
Belongs to somebody

When I walk down the street I see people laughing at me
I see people shaking their heads
Hey
That's that nigger's mama ain't it
Apple don't fall too far from the tree
They ought to lock her up
Hell she raised him
Yes I raised him
But you taught him how to steal not me

13

You put a joint in his mouth and a forty ounce in his hands
And told him it was all good
It's not my fault
I did everything humanly possible any mother could do
I prayed
I preached
I even beat my boy's behind every time
I thought he needed it
But my child succumbed
Falling for the oke-doke in the streets
Listening to the niggers
His homeboys
His partners
I won't give up on him
I won't turn my back
'Cuz he's mine
He's my gift
He's my child
He's still my son

There is an African proverb used loosely today
It takes an entire village to raise a child
But somebody down in the village
Felt they could do better than I
But he's still my one
And he's my only son

THEY SAID

(To friends of the sheltered children in Kenya)

They said I was nobody
They looked at the color of my skin
They looked in the community where I lived
They said my mama was a baby maker
And my father was missing in action
But they were just mouthing off
Trying to make me feel bad about who I am

I am a child of Africa
A leader of today
A mover and a shaker of tomorrow

I am your future scientist
I am your future doctor
I am your future lawyer
I am somebody
I am somebody

And what they say will never bother me
And what they say
Will never affect my destiny
Because I am somebody

MERRY CHRISTMAS DADDY

It's Christmas time and my thoughts are focused on you
I wanted you but you didn't want me
I've been looking for love all of my life
From boyfriend to boyfriend
From man to man
Jumping from one bed to the next
Trying to find a solution to this indescribable loneliness
I wanted you but you didn't want me

My heart ached for you
I turned corners in my life that were deadly
I should have been dead a long time ago
I made some hasty mistakes
I made myself do things that were crazy
I kept trying to fill the glass that was half full

Sometimes I cried
Asking God how could you walk away from me
I kept calling your name but no answer
I wanted to write you letters
But there was no address
I wanted to call you but there was no phone

You pushed me out of your life and I hated you for that
I wanted peace in my heart
I wanted peace in my mind
I wanted to find safety in your arms
But you turned your back on me

There were times when I would see you
You would say
Look I did the best that I could do
But your excuses left me uncovered

16

I was molested
Rejected
I was promiscuous
I was confused and needy
I was a cocaine queen
An alcohol fiend
I was helpless and reckless to myself
You left me alone

It was your job to teach me how a man should treat me
It was your job to teach me how a man should respect me
It was your job to teach me how a man should love me

So Daddy this piece is for you
Your ignorance became my brilliance
I went through hell as God held my hand
I walked on water and never drowned
See Daddy you left me
But God kept me

Merry Christmas to you Daddy
Peace and blessings to you
And a special blessing to fathers all over the world
Who understand the importance
Of loving their precious baby girls

Merry Christmas Daddy
I hold no grudge against you
In fact I forgive you

MAMA AT THE BURIAL SITE

They said I shouldn't be mad at you
They say you are the victim and not the perpetrator
But you pulled the trigger
You are the one who took him out
Pumping his body full of lead
He never knew what hit him

His face stained with blood
His eyes protruding
A look of surprise gleamed across his face
Why
Because you were the surprise that took him out

Ya'll grew up together
Lil' shorties running around the 'hood in mischief in play
He never bothered nobody
An excellent student and his future was bright
He played basketball and oooh how that boy loved to dance
The girls called him the chocolate prince

But you took him out and I'm not supposed to be mad
'Cause you're the victim and not the perpetrator
I shouldn't hate you
I should forgive you
I should be super human
Super Christlike
Ms. Empty my bleeding heart and see the misguided boy
Who fell through the cracks

So what he killed my baby
So what he killed my child

It's not his fault

The boy never knew his father
And his mama worked most of the time
His mama never had no time for her son
This was a community child
The streets just swallowed him up
It's not his fault
He's the victim and not the perpetrator

Standing at his grave site
Internment resembles judgment
'Cuz like God
I'm mad as hell
And somebody got to pay a price eternally
Ashes to ashes and dust to dust
Ashes to ashes and dust to dust

I feel my breath begin to stagger
Rage fills me like explosives
I wanna hurt somebody
Better yet I'd rather kill somebody

Leave me alone and let me fill my pain
Don't tell me what to feel
Don't tell me not to hate
Don't tell me I can't take a life for a life

Ashes to ashes
Dust to dust
Ashes to ashes dust to dust

Good night my chocolate prince
Sweet dreams
Mommy loves you
But God loved you best

Ashes to ashes and dust to dust
Good night my son
One day I shall see you in the morning

ODE TO COLTRANE

John Coltrane says let us pursue him on the righteous path
Yes it is true
Seek and ye shall find
God help us to resolve all of our fears and weaknesses
Because through you God all things are possible

As he plays his saxophone he talks to God without words
Each note was a word to him
That was greater than ourselves
Oh yes Coltrane knew God
It was the sound of each note
Coltrane called out to God in a musical language
No one knew the conversation but Coltrane and God
Coltrane knew how to vibe with God
He had a language all to himself
You couldn't understand his words
But you could feel his music
And in your soul there was a stirring
And you screamed "blow Coltrane, blow"

Blow to him who created the foundation of the world
Blow to him who says:
I am God and there is none like me
I am the beginning
I am the end
I speak mysteries and some you will never understand
To know me is to love me
To love me is to understand me
To understand me is to surrender to me

Coltrane captivated God's attention
With his magical melodies and rhythmic runs
In a rapturous zone of hear me God too

During this time of spiritual delusion
Where everybody wants to preach
And folk appear more crazy than factual or knowledgeable
I thank God for this one thing
That I know him for myself
Doesn't matter to me what people preach
I know the great I Am for myself
So like Coltrane
I too talk to God
In a language nobody understands
Except the spirit of Brenda
And the mind of God
In a language
In a rhythm
In a voice
That only God understands
Like Coltrane the jazz man
Who ministered to God and he listened
In a language
In a rhythm
In a voice
That only God understands

You better learn to stop listening to
Neophyte
Fanatical
Spiritualists who think they know the truth
And learn how to find God for yourself
Like Coltrane the jazz man
Who ministered to God and God listened
In a language
In a rhythm
In a voice
That only God understands

Find your voice in God
And get to know him
For yourself

Like Coltrane the jazz man

A RESURRECTION MAN

Dedicated To The Men Of The Resurrection Missionary
Baptist Church

(Uncle Pete, Thanks for being you...)

Like the old time prayer warriors he says
I'm gon' place my sword in the sands of time
And I ain't gon' study war no more

A resurrection man
Walks in the favor of God
He is anointed, appointed and ready to do the will of God
Like Jacob he is a wrestler
Lord I won't let you go until you bless me

A resurrection man is a tithe payer
A foundation layer
A kingdom builder
And a team player

A resurrection man lives by the word of God
Because the steps of a good man are ordered by him

A resurrection man knows the vision of his pastor
He works with him and not against him
Because a house divided will never stand

Like Jeremiah weep over God's people
And warn them of such a time as this
Like Elijah prophesying at all times
Like Abraham remember the covenant of your blessing

Go forward resurrection man
The enemy knows and he can see
That a resurrection man will die on his feet
Because he who the son has set free
Will never be defeated at the hands of the enemy

SISTAH'S MISSING THE POINT

I think sometimes my Sistah's miss the point
So what you had sex in fifty different positions
And you can make your vaginal walls clamp down
So hard on his rod of stamina
He sang lift every voice in eight different languages

So what
You came
He came
Ya'll came together
While driving down 69th Street

You made love on satin sheets covered in soft rose petals
He sensually massaged your body from head to toe
As you ate chocolate covered strawberries while sipping
champagne

But here's a dash of reality
Your home phone's been off for months
But his cell phone is on and you my Sistah pay his bill
You claim he's paying your bills and keeping your rent paid
But in the same breath your children are complaining
Ain't no food in the house
It's funny he has the pin number to your cash card
And you can't understand why all your checks keep bouncing

And you keep telling the world
How you get laid to get paid
Looks like you're getting played to me

You love him more than you love yourself
You cater to him
More than you cater to the needs of your children
Your happiness is making him happier
You tell him you love him
He tells you
"I LIKE YOU A LOT"

Girl get off Fantasy Island
You are a woman of beauty
A gift presented to the world by God himself
So be careful who you let open your package

Making love is beautiful
It is spiritual
It's a sacred act between you and your husband
Not between you and your man
'Cuz your man keeps playing in your panties for free
But your husband knows he that finds a wife finds a good thing

TALES FROM A BATTERED WOMAN

Broken bones and disfigured faces
Twisted lies and half spoken truths
I heard him say he loved me
I heard him say he would never be mean to me
Because I was his queen

London bridge is falling down
Falling down
My fair lady

No Not Again
He promised he would never hit me again
Facial bones crumble
His fist strikes my face like a bulldozer
Tearing into an abandoned building
I fall while blocking brutal blows preparing for the next

He kept screaming at me like I was a stranger
Get up
Get your behind up right now
I told you when you got outta line
I would beat you down

He loves me
He loves me not
He loves me
He loves me not

You're just stupid
You never get it right the first time do you

Love shouldn't hurt
Or impair
Or beat down
Love shouldn't violate
Or judge
Or oppress
Love should not ridicule or control or deceive

Love nurtures
Love understands
Love is patient and kind
Love listens
I said love listens
How long will you take my heart
Take my sincerity
Take my trust
Running with my life in your hands
Making people think I'm hallucinating
What I know to be true

I hate you
Yet I sit here immobile scared to leave your wicked behind
I'm screaming at God
Let me go God
Let me get up and walk out that door right now

And just like I ask God is what he did
But I couldn't go
I will never make it by myself
Why should I leave
I learned how to take a beating
My daddy beat my mama
My granddaddy beat my grandma
They never left so why should I
Everybody screaming at me

But nobody is listening to me
I need help
I need healing
I need refuge

I need to listen to the voice of her crying out on the inside
There's a new you on the inside let her out
Let her out
Then strength will come
And brand new directions will follow
If I let her come on out

THE SEDUCTION

The moon shimmers in the heat of the night
I look up and count the stars
Holding my hand tightly we walk in synchronized rhythms
The ocean splash dances around our feet

Reaching out you take me into your arms
Lightly your tongue rolls to find hidden erogenous zones
Making me moan in the midnight
Your hand caresses my breast
And you kiss me in all the secret places

As I call out your name
Each time encourages you more to tantalize
To tease
To touch
In my ear I feel your breath
I even feel your heart beat

I hear you say lay down baby lay down
Without hesitation you lay me down in the sand
I close my eyes
And listen to the waves crashing against the rocks
The sensation of the water takes me to another level
I prepare to take all of you inside of me
Wordless screams fill the night air
This feels so good please never let me go

Climax burst like erupting volcanoes
Our bodies tremble
Dancing to the melodies we made
The water continues rushing between us
I wish this night would last forever

The night ends
And we walk away in the shadows of the moonlit night
Reflection always brings smiles of complete satisfaction
I only wish for one change
I wish we had used condoms
But many times we don't think we just do

But how do you stop passion
How do you control lust
When love feels right I just do it
Rather than second guest my man's trust

I REMEMBER

The Voices of 7th and 8th Grade Students from North Lawndale and Englewood

(God help us as adults to open our blind eyes)

I remember when I was six and my grandma taught me my *ABC's*

I remember when my mama used to listen and talk to me

I remember when my cousin and I would play in the back of my house

I remember when my daddy got shot

I remember I used to run while I was getting a whipping

I remember the last time someone tried to make me join a gang

I remember when my daddy beat my stepmother

I remember my cousin and me watching our parents get high and thinking how we wanted to try it

I remember when my brother didn't sell drugs

I remember the first time I gave up on my dreams

I remember when sticks and stones would break my bones
But words wouldn't hurt me

I remember when my friend got shot in the head playing
with something he shouldn't have been playing with

I remember the first building they tore down
I remember just sitting there thinking what could we have
done to avoid this

I remember the first time my daddy wrote me from jail

As I read these poems I remembered the words of Jesus

Blessed are the poor in spirit for theirs is the kingdom of
heaven

Blessed are those who mourn for they shall be comforted

Blessed are the meek for they shall inherit the earth

Blessed are the pure in heart for they shall see God

Blessed are the peacemakers for they shall become the
children of God

WHEN WE MET

When we met I was 16 and he was 20
Tall and built to perfection
His eyes sparkled like stars at midnight
His smile would break any woman's heart
He was my man and I loved him unconditionally

We had the kind of love
That you read about in romance novels
He was my life skills teacher
And I was his education for life student
The more we talked the deeper our love became

He was older but I was mature for my age
He was in college always talking about his career
He knew everything and I trusted him
Even if it meant my life I would lay it down for him

The boy knew how to make love to me
To my mind
To my body
To my spirit

When we made love it was spiritual
The heavens opened and the angels applauded
And I believed that even God himself smiled

In this brother I saw no wrong
I thought he was definitely sent to me by God
He was my lover
My prince
My confidant

One time while we were making love
He said softly
He said gently as he held and caressed me
He said baby will you live in this moment with me
Will you forget about everything and just trust me

I closed my eyes and he held me tightly
He rocked me in the cradle of his arms
I screamed his name
And like magic we came together

He was my first love and I was only sixteen
I gave him my all
I gave him everything
He was my knight in shining armor
He was my hero
He was my best friend

Truly I will never forget him
The man I trusted with my life
Took my life
You better be careful when someone says
Live in the moment with me
Be careful when he says trust me baby trust me
In that moment
You could become just like me
Infected and living with HIV

Now I watch the days go by
Till it's my turn to die
He was my first love and I was only sixteen

WAITING ON BOAZ

I was told why should a man buy the cow
If he gets the milk for free
As women we keep complaining where are the men
Somebody send me a soldier
I'm not Destiny's Child
But I'm a woman waiting to meet my destiny

I made a decision a long time ago to just say no
I was waiting for my king
Like Sister Ruth I was waiting for Boaz to find me
I decided to honor God with my body
And that meant abstinence
So I put my drawers on the alter right next to Jesus
So I could please God and stop pleasing the brothers

I was a temple hoe
Continuously lying about
How I was saved single and satisfied
Shouting on Sundays
And backing that thang' up on Mondays
I fell short and let God down
Singing rejection ballads
As I lay in lonely beds
Crying on tear stained pillows
Feeling sorry for myself
And I like the fact that God ignored me
It was time to make a choice
It was time to do the right thing

My flesh is a test and my faith is the key
My obedience is what God sees
So I'll wait
And when God says yes

I won't have to look for Boaz
Boaz will find me
Because he that finds a wife finds a good thing

CHANGE

Life is sometimes cloudy
Unsure
Misdirected and misunderstood
And I walk around stumbling
And fumbling trying to find my way
I keep hurting but can't tell where the pain is coming from
I want to turn back but I can't

I wear a mask and I wear it well
Nobody can know that I goof
That I'm human and that I make mistakes
Nobody can know when I close my bedroom door that I cry
Nobody can know that my heart hurts and that I struggle

I'm supposed to dream
As winners call my name
And I step up to the plate and receive the prize
But I chose to stay
In my place of comfort

But change calls out to me
Like crystal blue waters
And cloudless skies
Like green grass growing in the wintertime

Change calls out to me like the cry of a newborn baby
Like the voice of a father returning home
Change calls out to me
Like the crack addict who throws away her pipe
Like the gangbanger who throws down his gun
Like the troubled child who frees himself
And walks in the sunshine

If I want something I've never had
I have to do something I've never done
And that is to believe in myself
To put the past behind me
To step out of the old and step into the new

No more anger
Where I hurt myself
And others around me
Change
It's a place I've never been
But it's a place I think I'll stay

MS. MATTHEWS

Dedicated To Brenda Matthews by Angela Parker
8th Grade Ericson Elementary

Ms. Matthews is a pearl

Ms. Matthews is a dime

Ms. Matthews is a mother figure who understands me all
the time

Ms. Matthews is a queen to whom I always dream

Ms. Matthews is a mentor for whom I will always pray for

Ms. Matthews is a woman who loves everything going and
coming

Ms. Matthews has every characteristic a woman should
have

When I become a woman

I will have those characteristics too

But first she encourages me to stay in school and do what I
need to do

ADDICTION AFFLICTION

Satisfying my addiction and when it's over I wanna die
Knowing my actions are wrong
Understanding in my conscience this verb needs to stop
But I can't seem to stop it
It controls me and I like it
My mouth says this is wrong but my body says
Sister girl help yourself

I know what it's like to smoke cigarettes
Till your chest hurts and your throat gets sore
Chain smoking putting one cigarette out
And minutes later lighting another
I know what it's like
To make love to the refrigerator
Eating till there is no more room
But like a good orgasm
There is always room for one more

Addiction affliction
Taking control like a nasty virus
That uncontrollable place that feels good
The hidden place that you always tell God you want to stop
But you can't
At least that's what your mouth says

Like the heroin addict who stands in the blow line
With his last ten dollars
 Saying to himself
I control the blow
The blow don't control me
Besides he says
Hell
I just like to get high

And though ten dollars represents the last of his paycheck
He stands in the blow line
Like a proud soldier going off to war

Addiction affliction
We crying out to God
But God ain't listening 'cuz we still playing

Addictions stay hidden in the dark
They are safe in the secret place
But if we allow the light to shine
And expose the secret places
Darkness can't live in the light
Then the addictions would become exposed
And soon fade away

SOMEBODY BETTER SAY SOMETHING

My eyes cry salty tears
My soul yearns to see something different
But reality is what it is
Who do we blame
Whose fault is it

I walk down Westside streets
With broken beer bottles and whiskey bottles under my feet
As glass and garbage replace flowers and grass

The 2900 block of West Lexington
Had become the dope express
Cars block the streets stopping traffic
As heroin and crack consumers
Make their way to the Wal-Mart of dope spots

A better bang for your buck
A bigger blow for your nose
Ready rock
Ready rock
Just park stop and blow

We got churches on every corner
And lots of Arabs' stores too
The police
Right up the street

And liquor stores
That have something for the whole family
Half pints and forties
For those who like cocktails
After a day of washing windshields
Or begging for loose change

We have *Tops*
Tops for the brothers and sisters who swear
That reefer is an herb
And will heal any sickness known to mankind
There is candy for the children
Milk for the babies
And Hoghead cheese
For those needing a quick snack

Somebody better say something
Somebody better do something
Somebody better feel something

Have we become numb
Have we choked in our own vomit
And died a hopeless case of
I don't care no more

Has fear locked up our minds
Are we once again bound by slavery
A slavery we created for ourselves
So we let our children die
With no explanation
Or no recourse

Somebody better say something
Somebody better do something
Somebody better feel something

We have families without fathers
We have families without husbands
We have families without men

We have children
Who never laid eyes on their daddy

45

Because it was never about the baby
But all about the booty call with daddy's boo

Now we have sisters having babies
Talking about I don't need a man
I'm gon' take care of me and mine

Yet we see these same sisters
On these stupid talk shows
Trying to prove paternity
Crying like a fool
Talking about I don't know
Who my baby daddy is
And you've done tested three on the show already

Somebody better say something
Somebody better do something
Somebody better feel something

We blow our money on casinos
On lotto's
We buy top shelf alcohol
We drive the fanciest cars
We wear the most expensive clothes
We've cornered the market
On five dollar rocks and ten dollar blows
Our boys have become ballers
And our girls
The rappers and the community
Calling them hoes

Somebody better say something
Somebody better do something
Somebody better feel something
Before it is too late

WHAT YOU TEACH ME

You have always taught me
Don't do as I do
But do as I say

But I say to you today
You have been a poor teacher
A poor example
A poor role model
And at times a poor parent

You want me to listen to your words
And ignore your actions
But your actions affect me
And the fate of my destiny

My first cigarette came from your purse
My first beer came from your refrigerator
I smoked my first blunt that was left in your ashtray
In the living room of our house where we live
Together

I learned to cuss
By listening to you
I learned to lie
Because you taught me too

Please take the time
And listen to me
Think about the words that you teach me
From where I stand
It's plain to me
You have never practiced what you preach

BACK IN THE DAY

Back in the day
We used to grind until midnight
To the sounds of Marvin Gaye
Who sang *Distant Lover*
And Earth Wind and Fire
Had R*easons*
The O'Jays
Took us *Up The Stairway To Heaven*

And don't forget about Sister Betty Wright
Who wrote and sang the national anthem
For all virgins across the country
Who wanted to rip off their drawers
And sing their song loudly and proudly
Tonight is the Night
That you make me a woman
You said you'd be gentle with me
And I hope you will

Betty Wright taught us to give it up
And turn it loose
We danced in dark musty basements
Under black lights
Where the walls would sweat
As teenagers congregated in huge numbers
In small spaces
We were in revival
And the church said yes
And the only thang' you had to pay
Was fifty cents to get in

And we danced
'Til sweat popped off our faces

And our clothes became wringing wet
And our mouths became sore
As we tongue kissed
And the boys played in our panties
And we moaned
Because we liked it
And we didn't care who watched
Because we all were doing the same thing

Back in the day
When we smoked reefer
In hidden places because we had respect for the elders

Back in the day
When we would shake and bake
White Port and Kool-Aid
Drinking in secret places because we were having fun
And we didn't wanna get in trouble

Back in the day
When we wore real platform shoes
With hot pants
And micro minis with white girl go-go boots
And palazzo pants
We were the generation
Who put 'Polly and Esther' on the map
We were the Psychedelic P Funk Nation

Back in the day
We were doing the Dog
With George Clinton
And did the Under Water Boogie with Bootsy Collins

We were young
Ballin' with the best
And not bothering nobody
We had each other's back
And would take up the slack
For one another

We sang songs on the corners
Had real barbeques in the back yards
With real grass
And real flowers
With real family and friends

Back in the day
We dreamed dreams
And had visions of success
We were gon' be somebody great
We went to church
Sang in the youth choir worked on the Usher boards
And even stayed for Holy Communion

Back in the day we loved God
And he was real to us
And it didn't matter if Jesus was black or white
Because we loved him unconditionally
And he loved us back
Back in the day
When we were real with ourselves
And we were real with each other

CASINO GRANNY

First I read my scripture
The wealth of the wicked
Is laid up for the righteous
Yes Lord
You're speaking to my soul today

Jesus said
Whatever you ask in my name
And do not doubt
I will give to thee
Then he went on to say
Search ye first the kingdom of heaven
And its righteousness
And all these other things will be added

Lord I thank you
For all your goodness
And you know what I stand in need of
You told me to never worry
That even the strands of my hair
Had been counted by you

So as I get ready for my journey
I'm asking you Lord for your blessings
Asking for your journey mercy
And Lord don't forget about your grace

Whew!!!
Lord you alright with me
As I put on my coat
Got my money in my pocket
I done said my prayers
Asked for God's blessings

And quoted my scriptures
Look at the time
I'm gon' be late
Last time people got to the church late
The bus left without 'em

I'm so glad that the church
Has put together
Different kinds of fellowship activities

You see the Lord didn't intend for us to
Stay inside the four walls of the church all the time
As Christians we are to go out
Evangelizing spreading the good news of the gospel
Even when we're out having fun

I used to go by myself
Now the whole church goes
I see so many people from the various churches
Almost like a non-denominational conference
There is Baptist
Catholic
Church of God in Christ
Evangelicals
Holiness
Assembly of God
Muslims
And Jehovah had a witness there too

The church has finally found something we all enjoy
Who would have thought
That the riverboat casino
Would attract church folk from all walks of life
I'm talking saved sanctified
Men and women of God who love the Lord

And it must be all right with God
'Cause my pastor goes with us
Last time he won fifteen-hundred dollars

That's why I take the Lord with me wherever I go
Even to the casino
'Cause if the pastor is winning
I know his flock got to win too

Who knows
Since we all fellowship on the riverboat
Soon we can have church services too
I don't see why the church don't build their own casinos
All in the name of Jesus
The Bible says
Ye have not 'cuz ye ask not
I see baptisms too

'Cause it's people on that boat who need Jesus
And we might as well spread the word while we're there
'Cause if you gon' play the game you should know
Who's gon' help you stay in the game
Nobody but Jesus
Excuse me while I sang my song

The ship is at the landing don't you wanna go
Oh yes
I want to go
Jesus make me a lucky lady tonight

CRACK GIRL SPEAKS

Standing on the corner
Not waiting for a bus or a cab
On a mission to soothe this urge
Snow falls like large blankets covering the streets

Standing here scarcely dressed
Watching each car that passes
My feet feel like cold blocks of ice
My nose running
My eyes watering
The wind cuts my body like angry daggers
Can't leave got to get this monkey off my back

The traffic light turns red
I look into the eyes of one
I smile and he nods
Into the car I go
Finding a vacant spot in the back of an alley
I'm on my knees again
Head bobbing
Tongue racing
Praying to God this brother won't try nothing stupid
Ten minutes pass
There it goes
The scream I've been waiting for
Pop goes the weasel

Wiping myself off
I take my money and get out the car
No thank-yous
I don't even look at him
Can't even tell you what he looks like

Making money all day long
Now time to head to the spot and cop
While walking down that dark alley
I reach into my pocket and pull out my pipe
Here in my hands is the love of my life
Reaching into my pocket
I find a few rocks still left from the last cop
So I stop in this abandon building and get my thrill on
Loading the instrument of my passion
With the rocks of my salvation
Lifting my instrument
My heart races
As I slowly and deeply
Inhale the destruction of myself
The demons surround me
I hear them talking to me

Smoke it girl
Smoke it
Get your row out
Hell you been waiting for this

As I keep loading the instrument of my passion
With the rocks of my salvation
I start thinking about my children
Haven't seen them in five days
Don't even know
If they're living or dead

But I'm Hungry
Tired
Dirty
Nasty

Wearing the same clothes

As the demons keep speaking to me
Smoke it girl
Smoke it

I have no more control
I lost myself after I took that first hit years ago
The first hit
There wouldn't be a last hit
If it wasn't for the first hit

Today I live my life as the rock star
The freebase queen
The dope diva
Ain't no shame in my game
Living my life on my knees
And on my back
As the demons keep speaking to me
Smoke it girl
Smoke it

What happened to my dreams
What happened to my success
What happened to my life
Where was that road to freedom leading me to greatness
It all sat in the hands of my own condemnation
The instrument of my passions
The rocks of my salvation
The voices of self now controlled by the demons
Who called me out by first name

The cold wind whispers
Through the walls of this abandon building
Time to move on
The last hit had been smoked
The demons call for me

Back to the streets
And the demons know me by my first name
First hit
Wouldn't be a last hit if
It wasn't for the first hit

If I could say
If I could speak to my children
If I could speak to my brother and my sister
If I could speak to my babies
I would tell them stop the first hit
Please
Stop the first hit
Because the last hit
It never ends
It never
Ever ends

DEAD MEN WALKING

Eight million homeless walks the streets of America
Like wounded soldiers
Their blood wasted
As never ending battles continue
No rescue teams come to aid these soldiers

Persecuted for having nothing
Stepped on
Stepped by
By human beings
Images of themselves of what used to be

Viewed by many as
Worthless
Ignorant
Helpless beggars
Who want nothing

Yet these wounded soldiers
Stay in the battle everyday
Hoping
Wanting
Praying
That this war will soon end

Their clothes saturated with invisible blood
From broken hearts
Blood that runs free
Stepped on
Stepped by
By human beings
Images of themselves of what used to be
Drafted into this hell

Without consent
Hand picked

The soles of our shoes covered in their blood
As broken hearts cry for mercy
Stepped on
Stepped by
By human beings
Images of themselves of what used to be

In my spirit
I keep hearing these words
When you do it to the least of these
You do it unto me

Eight million dead men walking
Wounded soldiers
With broken hearts
Stepped on
Stepped by
By human beings
Images of themselves of what use to be

MY FIRST MAN

I sat down as the mood had been set
There was a hush all through the house
The light from the candles
Made abstract images throughout the room

Relaxing my body
Slowly I began to exhale
Not wanting to rush
Sitting silently and patiently
I waited for him
I felt a brush of fresh air come across my forehead
I closed my eyes
His presence was one I could not describe
This man was awesome
He was majestic
A king
Larger than life
He was the only one
Who could make me go inside myself

I kept my eyes closed
There was a comfort level in him
I trusted him
Heart mind and body

I was consumed by this man
With tears rolling down my cheeks
Shaking hands under my chin
Gently I said to him
I love you
I love you more than life itself

See intimacy was the key
I had been hurt over and over again
During the course of my life
Because I always picked the wrong man
Lovers
Who laughed at me
Leaving me listless
Lonely in lust
With my heart speaking won't somebody love me please

But this man was different
Better than the rest
He was my treasure
I had found my pot of gold
And I was rich in him

I told him again
I love you
Because you accepted me for me
In you I could be naked and never ashamed
Whenever you saw me
You would call me beautiful

You didn't care about my scars
Or my past mistakes
Or even that I had lived my life recklessly

All you wanted was to wipe away my tears
To release my fears
Hold me in your arms and never let me go

I told my friends all about you
They laughed at me
Girl ain't no man that good
He must be hiding something

Keep on he will hurt you just like the others
As I sit here in your presence
Your love is strong
Intoxicating
Addictive
I just wanna
I just wanna come and sit in your lap
And let you cast a spell on me
Now that I have you I will never leave you

Should the winds cease to blow
Should the stars fall from the sky
Should the sun fold up and never shine again
I will love you forever
Wherever you go I will follow
There is no mountain too high
No valley too deep
No river too wide that can ever separate me from you

I then said to this man
Can you please tell me your address again
He replied heaven
I said thank you God
He said I am your first man
I can fulfill you like no other man

He said
Feed the spirit first
Because as long as you live in the lust of the flesh
Your destiny will always be
The long-lasting pains of the past
Pains that would have never happened
If I had been your first man

HE GRANTS ME PEACE

He grants me peace
In the midst of the storm
He grants me peace
As time goes on
He grants me peace
In a world
Gone wrong
He grants me peace
When I'm not strong

I'm looking for him

On September 11th
The walls of Jericho
Came tumbling down
Terrorist attacks
Suicide bombings
Anthrax scares

And Wall Street dictates
While the White House eliminates
And corporations eradicate
While families lie prostrate

I'm looking for him

I ask the question
Do we die
Or do we try
To look for him

He said trust me
Do not doubt me

I will not forsaken you
I will not leave you
Don't you know I died for you
Red was the color of my blood
As I cried for you

You are my people
And I am
Your daddy God

If you speak
I will listen
While you walk
I will talk
While you run
I will cause the sun
To light your path
While you sing
I will make new melodies
To ring out in your heart

Come on now
I'm daddy God
I created the sun
The moon and the stars
I created the lilies of the field

I will give you peace
I will give you great days
Without heartaches and pains
I will lift up bowed down heads
Because you are covered in my blood
And my blood is red

Red was the color of my blood
When I cried for you
Red was the color of my blood
When they beat me for you
Red was the color of my blood
When I hung on the cross for you
Red was the color of my blood
When I screamed out to my father
It is finished for you

Not only did I die for you
I got up for you
And right now
I'm interceding just for you
And soon I'm coming back
Just for you

So my peace
My peace
I give to you

GIRL WHAT ARE YOU LOOKING FOR

I keep asking the question
What are you looking for
Everybody says
You just young dumb and full of come
A hoodrat
Giving away her kitty
To any fat cat
Who wanna play in her panties

Word on the street is
You'll do anything to make a dollar
So the brothers holla'
And you follow

Girl what are you looking for
On your knees
Trying to please your man
Do you really think
That sucking a man's penis
Will make you his number one woman
And he'll be your number one man

Walking the street
With your cell phone
Thinking you grown
Fake girls
With fake nails
Fake hair
Acting like fake females

What's your purpose
Tell me your destiny
Tell me where is your place in history
Who do you admire
What do you aspire to do

Like Fannie Lou Hamer
Will you awaken the sleeping giants
Will you lift your voice as an instrument of praise
And let your light shine

Like Sonia Sanchez
Will you write the struggles of your people
Will you tell of the battles
Will you wage war with your pen
Writing in red ink
Symbolizing the deaths of all the sisters
Who have fallen
But they call on you
They died for you
So you got to make it through

So while 'erbody in the club
Getting tipsy
You get busy
Writing your history
Writing your dreams
Like Pearl Cleage
Be mad at Miles
Like Maya Angelou
Know *Why The Caged Bird Sings*
Like Ntozake Shange
Find God in yourself
And love the Him in you

The question is
What are you looking for
And no one can answer the question for you
Sister girl only you know for sure

WHO IS HE?

I wanted to know him
I wanted to chase him
I wanted to get down with him

Like the fornicator getting down with her lover
My emotions
My hormones
My flesh on edge
Eagerly expecting
And waiting
I wanted him
I hungered for him

Like the junkie
Who filled his syringe
And slapped his arm
And found the vein
I wanted to go deeper in him
I wanted to be high in him
I wanted to close my eyes in him

Like the wine head
Stumbling
Staggering
Mouth watering
Wrapping his lips around his liquid god
I wanted to drink him
I wanted to taste him
To be filled with him
To become drunk with him

Like the baby who cried for his mother
I was looking for El-Shaddai
The anointed one
The multi-breasted one
I was the one
Who wanted to be
One-on-one
In his presence

I wanted to lie down prostrate
Face down
With tears streaming down my face
I wanted to scream his name
I could be naked and not ashamed

Like a prostitute needing a john
Like a murderer needing a gun
Like a thief with stolen goods
Like a hungry child with no food
Like a rich man with all of his money
Like the poor man always with nothing

I wanted to find you
In your presence
I could get down with you
You made me just like you
I can do anything
You empower me to do

In your presence
There are no pressures
Life worries
Or pain
In your presence the enemy has no gain

In your presence I will hear from you
In your presence a fresh anointing comes too
In your presence it's all about you
Magnifying and glorifying you
With my lips I will sing praises unto you

That's why I chase him
That's why I get down with him
That's why I love him
That's why I'll never ever leave him

I WENT TO VOTE TODAY

I went to vote today
I exercised my right
My civic duty
To have my say
In the democratic process

I'm not a patriot
But I must do what is right for the sake of my country

You laugh
Because I took out the time
To try and better life
For the sake of my children
For the possibility
Of an improved quality of life

No
I'm not a patriot
I'm not whistling Dixie
For a country
Who said my ancestors were 3/5ths of a human being

I voted today
Instead of staying home
Complaining
I got up
Got dressed
And cast my ballot

How shameful
The people
Who never voted in their lives
But have the nerve to complain

Talking 'bout
Politicians
Are liars
They're cheaters
They're stealers
They are self-righteous
Self-centered men and women
With their own ideas and hidden agendas

I voted today
I voted because Fannie Lou Hamer was beaten
I voted because Medgar Evers was shot in the back
I voted today because Harriet Tubman ran
And Fredrick Douglas refused
To be beaten down by the white man

I voted because my grandmother
Didn't have proper healthcare
I voted for the sixteen-year-old who is still in eight grade
I voted because of the sixteen-year-old
Recovering crack addict
I voted today
Because I wanted to lift every voice and sing
Because I wanted Umoja to ring
Because I wanted Kujichagulia to say my name

I voted for the hundreds
The thousands that died
I voted for the black man
Hung in front of his family
Because he dared
He attempted
He tried
I voted today
Did you

IT'S CALLED SCHOOL

If you didn't know
It's called school
The place where you learn and study
The place where you increase your knowledge
The place where you think about your careers
The place where you think about college

Listen
It's called school
Not the dating game
Or the place to play
With your friends

Not a place to hang out and get high
The place where you skip class
Not trying to pass
Just sitting around
Talking trash about the teacher

Listen
It's called school
Not the place for
Haterade sippers
Blunt smokers
Runners
Chicken heads
And bust downers
Wannabe' Mackers
And pimp masters
This is not the place
For gangsters or hustlers

No my people
It's called school
Not a place for fools
Not a place for hard ups
Who keep slipping up and giving up on themselves

This is the place where brain stimulation
Increases one's motivation
To complete your education
So there should be no hesitation
Because you have an obligation
In making the right choice

So in June
We shall see
Who were the real playas
And who were just the wannabe's

LIL' SALLY

Little Sally Walker
Sitting in a saucer
Rise Sally rise
Wipe your weeping eyes
Put your hands on your hips
And let your backbone slip
Oh shake it to the east
Oh shake it to the west
Oh shake it to the one that you love the best

Little Sally always knew
How to shake her fine brown thang'
Mama always told Sally
Baby beauty is in the eye of the beholder
And any man who saw Sally
Saw God

Sally could make a strong man plead
And make a righteous man
Throw away his Bible
Screaming Lawd have mercy on me

Sally said her coochie
Was tighter than that
Strap tied on a junkie's arm
So he'd go higher

You best believe
Sally knew how to do the do
She was an old man's dream
And she could make a young man come
Before he even got some

Sally didn't play
Any man who played in Sally's panties
Knew that the candy wasn't for free
Any man who played in Sally's panties
Paid handsomely

You see Sally had a secret
And with naked eye you couldn't see
That Sally was a sister
Infected with HIV
See
When Sally got the package
It pissed her off
And she vowed
Every nigger she knew would pay the cost
So my brothers
Sally's coochie
May feel like sweet sunshine
But coming in Ms. Sally
May end the rest of your lifetime

Oh shake it to the east
Shake it to the west
Shake it to the one that you love the best
Who you gon' give it to now Ms. Sally
Who's gon' get it now!!!!!!

LOVE THY NEIGHBOR AS THYSELF

God said to love thy neighbor as thyself
To be just as concerned about others
To listen and respond to them
Not putting their problems on a shelf

This issue is real to me
I wish the President
Would honor God's request
To love thy neighbor as thyself

Mr. Bush
It was said
That you are a Christian man
A godly man
A family man
A man who knows
All about morals and values
A man who would never compromise his position
When it came to addressing real political issues

But every time you use your pen
It's the poor man who takes the fall again
The Bible says to love thy neighbor as thyself
But looks like the rich people of this country
Controls all the wealth
Including yourself

Jesus said it would be easier for a rich man
To go through the eye of a needle
Than a rich man to enter God's kingdom

I think Mr. Bush and the religious right
Have become shortsighted
The only difference between a rich man
And a poor man
Is wealth

But God said to love thy neighbor as thyself
Mr. Bush you should follow
The examples of Christ
Jesus himself made many sacrifices
I'm not asking you to die on a cross
But you should recognize
People living in poverty suffers great loss
Healthcare
Living wages
Economic disparities
Housing
Poor education
Jobs and HIV

Yet in this country
We still see
Tax breaks and corporate welfare
For the nation's wealthy

Please President Bush take a good look
I think you need help
In understanding scripture
When it says to love thy neighbor as thyself

We are fighting a war that's insane
We can't find Bin-Laden
But locked up Hussein

Is America making sure
That Iraq becomes free
Is America making sure
Iraq becomes a democratic society

Now that's funny to me
When in this country
Democracy is nothing but hypocrisy
Engineered by poverty pimps
Who specialize in stealing presidential elections
Mr. Bush please honor God's request
Learn how to love thy neighbor as thyself

Instead of weapons of mass destruction
Let's share weapons of mass salvation
Our weapons are not carnal
But mighty through God

Let's bring our troops home
No more death
And destruction
No more loss of life

The Iraqi people will never be free
As long as the U.S. continues to occupy their country
It's time for change

President Bush
A new day is at hand
Help those who can't help themselves
Stop this war based on oil money and wealth
Stop your lying
Stop helping yourself
And learn how to love thy neighbor as thyself

MAE ALICE THE SLAVE WOMAN

God
Why have you turned a death ear to me
Standing here with chains around my neck
With chains around my feet
My back scarred from the master's whip
God you are my father
And I am your child
Open up the windows of heaven
And lean over the banisters in glory and hear your child

I was brought to this land on a ship
My destination unknown
Sailing for days losing time itself
Laying side by side
Each of us calling out to a power
That was greater than ourselves
Asking the question
Why

Upon reaching my destination
Little did I know my life would be forever changed
Here I stand in tattered clothing
My mind confused and my dignity lost
Brutally raped by seething task masters
Who find their crimes of passion just
Don't they know if you cut me I bleed
If you hit me I cry

Does the white man feel I am capable
Of degrading myself
For the purpose of him to glory in my shame
Publicly humiliated for all to see
Yet there resides in me an inner peace

I watched as they hung my husband from a tree
I birthed three babies into this world
Three different times
Never even heard my babies cry
I watched as they snatched each one right from my womb

I have been face to face with tragedy
Every since I stepped on the shores of this new land
But in the midst of my tragedy
I live by the words of Job
Though they slay me yet will I trust you

My prayer today God
Please set me free
And if freedom is not for me
Set my children free
And my children's children
So they may live
The abundant life you speak about in your word

So Lord as I stand
Here on this auction block
With blood stained tears
In tattered clothing
Over and over again
Raped and beaten
And bound by chains

I want you to know
Though they slay me
Yet will I trust you
They may kill my body
But they will never kill my spirit

MY PURPOSE

Before he ascended into heaven
He said go
Go ye therefore
And teach all nations
Baptizing them
In the name of the Father
And of the Son
And of the Holy Ghost

He told me to go
Go and spread
The good news
Of the gospel
I had to do it
This wasn't a summons
I was commissioned

He looked at me
He looked inside of me
He filled my soul
There could be no fear
I had to be bold

I had to save one more for Jesus
One more for him
Who had saved me
Sanctified me
The one who died for me
Took on my sins for me
How he walked through hell for me
Snatched the key
No more eternal damnation
I was set free

To live forever
With Jesus eternally

There was a process
To producing godly characteristics
So that I could reach out
To them that were lost
I had to go
Where I didn't wanna go
I had to do
What I didn't wanna do

I had to tell my story
Share my testimony
I had to reveal my dirt
I had to confess my mess

I couldn't do it alone
My isolation
Would bring about devastation
To my soul salvation
So I found exhortation
Which brought about a manifestation
Of worshipping him

I was made to worship him
To have fellowship
To serve
Finding my place in ministry
To evangelize
Making disciples
To set humanity free

God used my body
To tell his story
So I'm balling for Jesus
So that he gets the glory

I will clench my fist
I will grit my teeth
I will tell the devil to his face
You can't have me

I'm on a mission
And God's got his hands on me
I'm kingdom building
As he enlarges my territory
I crossed over
And found my purpose

And my purpose is to serve
To make sure God's voice is heard
My purpose is to plant his seed
Utilizing my spiritual gifts
My talents and natural abilities
My purpose is to take Jesus to the streets
So that all people
From all walks of life are set free
And in the end
I shall live with my Jesus eternally

ROCKS AND BLOWS

There he stands in the parking lot of the grocery store
Tall with broad shoulders
Caramel colored skin and melting eyes
Strong arms waving in the winds
Making gestures
To all that passes him by

Who is he
I hear his voice rumble like midnight thunder as I passed by
His echoes filled the air
A constant flow of words fell from his lips
He made sure his words flowed freely
With great definition and piercing sound

His high cheekbones and thick darkened lips
Evolved his traits of African descent
Nubian kings and African queens
Surrounding him was years of sorrow sweat pain and death
The keys to life had been passed on to him
He was marked as the chosen generation

His life was to be a joyous experience
Passing on traditions from generation to generation
A beacon of light mesmerizing all who encountered
This handsome caramel colored brother
He was to lead his people
Out of the bondages of social injustice
He was the light
That would transform poverty into prosperity
Again he was marked as the chosen generation

But there he stands in the parking lot of the grocery store
He's not sending words of encouragement
Or educating his people on the plight of the black man
He's not standing there screaming
No justice
No peace
He's screaming

Rocks and blows!!!

Rocks and blows!!!

My God there he stands screaming
Rocks, rocks and blows!!!

NOBODY CAME FOR ME

Since I was a little girl
I was taught how to give a head job
Now at age thirteen
For ten dollars
I'll give a head job now
My mama knows what I do
I told her all about it
My mama says baby take care of your business
'Cause your mama understands

Me and Mama we get high together
Drinking Cisco and smoking blunts

And my daddy he's a real trip
Because he's been molesting me since I was a little girl
At night I'd sleep with a lot of clothes on
Even my coat my hat and my shoes
Hoping when daddy sneaks in my room just maybe with
'alla these clothes on
This time he'll leave me alone

But…
He still forces himself on me anyway
He slaps his hand across my mouth
His body is so heavy I can barely breathe
He whispers in my ear you better not tell nobody
'Cause if you do I will kill you

So in between my daddy beating
My mama during the day
He'd have sex with me at night
School is a problem
I would stay up all night long

'Cause I knew daddy was coming in my room
So the only time I sleep is in school
I try to do the work but I can't
Now I pretty much stay where I can
Wherever
Whomever
'Cause if I go home
I already know what's going to happen
My mama can't do nothing
Most times he's beating her
Or they are getting drunk together
It's scary though
I have three other sisters under me
Which brings me back to
Yes I give head jobs
Yes I dress like a hoochie
Yes I shake my behind
And say all kinds of cuss words

No
I don't respect people and hell naw'
I ain't afraid to die
I died years ago at age six
My spirit died
The first time my daddy crawled on top of me
And I screamed
And I screamed
And I screamed
And nobody came for me

At age seven I was sending out S.O.S signals
Help me somebody
Please help me somebody
And again nobody came for me

Now
I'm the talk of the 'hood
Here comes that fast girl
The bust down
The slut
And you know what that doesn't bother me

What I care about is the next time
People hear a little girl scream
The next time people hear a child scream
The next time people hear a baby scream
Maybe they'll come for her
'Cause nobody ever came for me

Say brotha'
You got ten dollars
How old am I
Should it really matter

Because nobody came for me
Nobody came for me
Nobody ever came for me

PLAIN AND SIMPLE FOLKS

E.W. and Verna Ruth Simpson
Were their names
Hardworking
Simple folk with a zest for life
Living in the hills of Mississippi
In a little town called Indianola
A God-fearing husband and wife
With ten children
Renting the land on which they lived
Who raised everything from hogs to pole beans

E.W was a man who stood on the steps of truth
Faith was his trump card
Humility was his light
And God was his everything
Verna his wife
Proud
Tall in stature
Her Bible stood as her road map
And love twisted around her shoulders
And mercy knew her as a welcomed friend

Amidst the racial tension in Mississippi
E. W. taught his children
Respect all people
Fear nothing but God
Never take a back seat to no man
And if you're right stand on it

These were the days of tough times
Where food was scarce
And work lasted from sun up to sun down

Starting at age five many of the Simpson children learned
How to chop cotton
And farm the land
And even though times were hard and food was scarce
They never saw a day without food on the table
With clothes on their backs
And a roof over their heads
They didn't have everything they wanted
But had everything they needed
Verna always trusted God's word

And there was a scripture that rang through her head
I've never seen the righteous forsaken nor his seed
Begging for bread

As time pressed on the Simpson family headed north
It was time for opportunity
And E.W. seized the moment
Packed up his family and headed for new land
North of the Mississippi Delta

SOMETIMES THE RAIN WILL FALL

In this life
Some rain must fall
And life turns you every way but loose
And you ask the question
Why must I face adversity
Why must heartless circumstances become my lover
Should I always wave my hands in surrender

I have tasted struggle
I have washed my feet in the Pool of Siloam
I have eaten the bread of consequence
Now loose me

I gotta climb higher
And lean towards the call of God's mercy
My voice parched
From singing sad songs
With sad melodies
I keep walking
'Cause I hear freedom calling my name

Harriet Tubman called my name
She said baby
If you wanna win
You gotta learn how to fight
She said
Clench your fist
Raise your head high
For the night has ended
And you must strike while it is day

Sojourner Truth called my name
She said

Baby
If you wanna live
You got to learn how to die

Die to yesterday
Carry old baggage
To the sea of forgetfulness
And toss it

Don't let life's pitfalls
Break your spirit
You got to
Put on the whole armor of God
And declare who you are
And whose you are
I am love…I am life

I am the spirit of Dr. King
because I've been to the mountaintop
I am the daughter of Fannie Lou Hamer
'Cause I'm sick and tired
Of being sick and tired
I am the child of the middle passage
Where the sea swallowed me whole
Yet my sprit lives

So even though the rain falls
And the pitfalls come
Because I know who I am
And whose I am
I know the sun
Will come out
After the rain
And I will shine
I will shine again

REMEMBERING THE MILLION WOMAN MARCH

We are coming
We are coming
One million women
October, 25th
Philadelphia, Pennsylvania

A day of healing
It's about repentance
It's about resurrection
It's about restoration
It's about looking at ourselves
Making changes
And moving forward
On a righteous path

Leaving the past behind
All of the suffering
All of that which jaded our image
Dimmed our view
And blocked our light

We rise walking in unified rhythms
Lifting our heads and raising our voices
Singing with melodies of praise

We have come
We have come
Our change has come
And we heal
And we heal
From the inside
One million sisters
Together we heal on the inside

SOUL FOOD SUNDAYS

Soul food Sundays
Was sitting down to Sunday dinners
At my grandma's house on Sundays after church
It was my uncles
Removing suit jackets and taking off cuff links
And rolling up shirt sleeves
It was loosening ties

It was Ida taking off her tight girdle
It was Doris stepping out of those tight high heel
Pointed toe shoes
It was Shirley with runs in the feet of her stockings
It was grandma saying
I know you didn't wear that to church
And where is your slip at
You showing all your stuff
It was boy when was the last time you had a hair cut

It was talking about
Child
Rev. Honey
Know he 'sho 'nuff preached this morning
Whew!!!!
What a time we had
And the choir almost tore the church house down

Soul food Sunday
Was my Uncle James saying grace
Lawd we thank you for the food we're about to receive
May it be nourishment for our bodies
Bless the hands that prepared it
In Jesus name amen

And the food would start passing
Pass me some greens
Grandma please tell Sister
Not to take all the pig tails out the greens
I want some macaroni and cheese
Save me a chicken breast please
Ooooh who made this dressing
And where's the hot sauce for the chitterlings

Oh my gawd!!!
Granny made a butter roll
And peach cobbler too!!!

Hey where's the red Kool-Aid
And why ya'll always buying this cheap pop
Can we get some Pepsi in here next Sunday please

Soul food dinners
Were the sounds of family screaming at the children
Oooooh!!!
Cortez and Bianca wrestling in grandma's living room
Cortez!!!
Cortez!!!
When I take my fingers out these greens and cornbread
I'm gon' beat ya'll behind!!!

Soul food is the sounds of family
Eating
Talking
Gathering
And moving about

It was reminiscing about the past
Ya'll remember when Joe-Joe locked himself in the dryer

Or when daddy caught Shirley
Smoking cigarettes on the couch
Remember when little Debra broke
The fish tank with her fat head
The fish died but little Debra lived to tell the story

Soul food Sundays
Was bigger than the meal
It was the meal
What happened during the meal
And after the meal
It was living
It was loving
It was laughing
And learning
It was soul food
It was food pha' your soul

It was new schoolers
Learning old-schoolers' lessons
It was us together on the inside
And what happened on the outside didn't matter
It was about us together on the inside
I sure thank God
For soul food Sundays

TELL ME WHY

(For All of My Children)

Tell me why my name
Doesn't go down in history
For me being me
Tell me why you judge me
Yet you don't even know me

Tell me why
I'm searching
Hoping
And expecting

Can you tell me why I was born
In a community influenced by violence and guns
Why do brothers and sisters feel that
Peace is made out of steel
When peace should be still

Tell me why people look down on me
Frown on me
Clown on me
Talk about me
Treat me and trip on me
But always looking to receive from me

Tell me why
If I'm not wearing
Iceberg
Phat Farm
Sean Jean or Fubu
You can't get with me boo
Cause I don't get down like you do

Well here's the lick
See if you can get with this
God created me you see
My beauty lies on the inside
It's my inner mystery

I keep asking you why
And constantly
You keep telling me lies
The revolution is in me
It's the power that God gave me
To resurrect my people and my community

I'm on a mission
So like Mary J. Blige
Ain't no need for hateration
Cause I got a inclination
To bring devastation
To my black population
About the revelation
Given to me
By God himself

And the revelation is
I am your revolution
I am your tomorrow
I am the seed that will set you free

So when I ask you why
Stop telling me lies
I'm not death or blind
I can both hear and see
So tell me the truth
And the truth will set us all free

THE GIMME SOME BLUES

I need to say something
I should be ashamed but I'm not
So I will say it anyway

I am not perfect
And just for today
I wanna say it
I AM NOT CELIBATE

I'm a saved
Single and sanctified woman of God
But just for today
I wanna take my drawers off the alter

I wanna close my eyes
And just do it for a long time
I'm dreaming of having some fun
Yes.....
Today I wanna get my freak on

What's a sistah to do
When she gets
The I WANNA GET ME SOME BLUES

I WANNA GET ME A MAN
Hold on to him tight
I want him to kiss me all over
Make me scream all night
I want him to rock me baby
Rock me all night long
'CUZ soon I'm going to hell in gasoline drawers
I've got the GET ME SOME BLUES
Yes I've got the I WANNA GET ME SOME BLUES

I CRIED MY LAST TEARS YESTERDAY

Today I said good bye to yesterday
Today I made up my mind
I'm not gon' hurt no more
I refuse to cry anymore

Weeping may endure for a night
but joy coming in the morning
I'm going to wave my flag in surrender
And I won't study war no more

Today I kicked yesterday out of my house
I looked yesterday in the face
and I said you can't live here no more
Today you got to go
I don't wanna hear your sad goodbyes
Just leave
I've had some hard times
I've seen some tragic days
I've held on while standing on shaky ground

It was God who kept me when the gas was shut off
Grace kept me when the lights were shut off
My food pantry got low
But my children never saw a hungry day
I've never seen the righteous forsaken
Nor his seed begging for bread

When I almost let go
When my mind started to wander
When it seemed my heart split in two
I had a talk with Jesus and he said to me

Yesterday is history

Tomorrow is a mystery
And today is a present

So I packed up my emotional baggage
Dried up my tear stained eyes
I pulled off depression
I shook off frustration
I stomped on worry
And I cast out fear
God has not given us the spirit of fear
But of power love and a sound mind

So I cleaned up my house
And I put the devil out
Yesterday is gone forever
And I decided that it's today that really matters
So I cried my last tears on yesterday
I cried my last tears on yesterday

THE FATHERLESS FEMALE

Sometimes I get angry
I try to pretend it doesn't bother me
Basically
I have raised myself
You never came to see me

I know who you are
I look just like you
At night I cry
Asking God
Why won't daddy love me
Did I do something wrong
Mama said she never stopped him from coming to see me

How does a father deny his own child
How do you plant a seed and never nurture it
How does the birth of your daughter occur
And you never speak her name
Does your heart bleed
Have you no shame

When I look in the mirror you are there
When I talk I hear your words
When I walk it feels like you're right beside me
You were my first man
You were my first love
I was supposed to be daddy's little girl
We were supposed to walk on sandy beaches and pick out
seashells

I was supposed to bake
My first chocolate cake for you
On my new Easy Bake oven

That Santa brought me for Christmas
It was I who would call you daddy
When I fell and scraped my knee
And you wiped away my tears holding me tightly
'Cuz I could always find safety in you arms

On Valentines Day
I wanted to pick out special cards
And buy Fannie Mae Candies
Write you poems and tell you how much I love you
I wanted to tell you about my boyfriends
And hoped you would meet my husband
Walk me down the isle when I married
And shed tears of joy
Because you were letting your baby girl go

But that never happened
I was rejected at birth
And abandoned
Forever

Somebody explain how does a father abandon
His own child
How do you sleep at night
How do you function

Child support
Is a father
Who actually participates in the life of his daughter
This is bigger than your money
I need you
I am angry
Yet I pretend this doesn't bother me

The fatherless female
Making stupid choices
Looking for love
From losers just like you
And look at what happened Daddy
I'm a single mother
With a baby's daddy just like you

THE POOR PEOPLE GATHER

The poor people are gathering
No more weariness
With its oppression
No more struggles
And long-lasting periods of unrest

See them gather their babies
Their belongings
Their sons and daughters
Their families

They're headed towards freedom
To a land that loves
Respects
Understands
And believes in them

No longer will political pimps
Hold captive the people who built this country
People who worked
Who slaved
Who sacrificed
While the government makes them
Feel that the economic woes of this country
Are their fault

The poor folks are gathering
And they're headed towards freedom
They're headed to a place that cares about the babies
They're headed to a place
That puts the family first
They're headed to a place
Where justice is real

A place where jobs pay livable wages
And healthcare is not just lip service
For politicians who are up for re-election

The poor folks are gathering
Headed down a new path
Generating new ideas

Headed to a place
Where welfare means
Health
Happiness
And prosperity

See the masses prepare for the great exodus
They have put behind
The pain and the struggle
Nights of crying
The years of watching their children die in their arms
Die in the streets

The poor folks are gathering
No red carpets rolled out
And the Star Spangled Banner never played

The poor folks are gathering
This story
An epoch
Of what should have been

The poor folks are gathering
They are moving
But not towards freedom
They march towards death
Can't you hear their eulogies

Across this country
Their epitaph reads
America we gave you our best
And in return
You gave us war
Separated our families
Buried us financially
Divided us politically
And sentenced us to death

THE PRINCESS

They said I wasn't
Pretty e'nuff
When I think about it
That's how it got started

As a young sister
I would hear words like
You kinda' got a pretty face

Then the anthems of how fat I was
Would play in my mind
Over and over again

I was dateless manless and friendless to myself
As I looked in the mirror
I didn't like me
I hated me
I wanted the image I saw to disappear

She just ain't pretty e'nuff
So instead of loving myself
I wandered into a world
Of misplaced values
Boasting of sexual exploits
While repeating First John 1:9
Because God is going to forgive me

Nobody carried my books to school
Or bought me flowers
Or took me to the school dance
Nobody ever asked for my number
Or took me out to lunch
Or walked with me by the lake

Holding my hand
While reading me poetry
As the birds sang and the sun smiled

So since love wouldn't come to me
I found love for myself
So I thought
I sold my soul for love
I settled
I compromised for love
I had sex for love
I was date raped for love
I was rejected for love
I became somebody else for love

I put myself on the market
New clothes
New attitude
My makeup flawless
My hair impeccably laid
And fragrances fit for a goddess
I was big but beautiful

To what gain was this new me
I found losers for lovers
Recovering addicts
Addicted to alcohol
With bad attitudes
And Christian men
Who wanted to find the anointing
Between the sheets
Monday thru Saturday
And find Jesus on Sundays
Because God wanted us to consummate our love
I was on empty

Yet I kept trying
Why wasn't it my time
Where was my prince
I deserved a prince

And none of this would have happened
Had I first seen the princess
In the mirror
Instead of loving her
I looked for love
In all the wrong places

Every woman wants to find
And love her own prince
But how can she love her prince
Until she first learns to love the princess

THE SILVER FOX

(For Totie Simpson and Verlee Jackson)

There's this wonderful lady who lives two houses down
I call her the silver fox
She thinks fast and cautiously reacts
Her silver hair
Reveal the autumn of her years
A woman of strength
Standing as a vanguard for her family

I see her all the time
She sits in a big chair
Near the living room window
Smiling at anyone who walks or drives by
She's a witty sister
Charming anyone who comes into her presence

The silver fox often tells stories of the old days
Growing up in the South
Working in the cotton fields
Raising a large family
Learning how to make little go a long ways

The silver fox is a God-fearing woman
She and God have this unique thang' going on
She talks to him
She tells him everything
And God being a just and righteous guy
Always comes to the rescue

As each day passes
Looking out the window in her big chair

She should see the trees wave in the winds
The flowers blooming
Or the sun lighting up the skies

Instead her heart bleeds
At the reality she really sees
Staggering drunks
Gangs running
People who drive by
And tute heroin in plain view
Kids dying
Mothers crying

What's amazing is that the silver fox doesn't get mad
Scream out the door
Or call the police
She just sits
And talks to God

There is a saying
The reason why most of us still live
Is because of the prayers of someone else

So instead of complaining
The silver fox just keeps on praying
And the nation keeps on changing
Because she believes in a God
Who keeps on saving
And we as a people keep on living

A KID'S PLEA

I am sick and tired of parents
They don't listen
They just scream and holler

So what do I do
I simply shut them out
If you can't talk to me
Like I'm a human being
Then I refuse to listen to your screaming
'Cuz I'm pleading I need you

Did it ever occur to you
That words hurt me too
Do you realize when you scream at me
You're actually screaming at you
I am a carbon copy of you
A designer's original
Especially made by you

My grandma always said
An apple don't fall too far from the tree

I am you
I am a reflection of you
I'm not perfect
I'm not who you want me to be
But I'm who I wanna be
And I need you to accept me for me

Talk to me
Understand me
Spend some time with me
Wrap your arms around me

And tell me you love me
Don't make me hide from you
I'm tired of running away from you
Many times I'm confused
Because it's impossible to talk to you
So I go to the streets and get what I need
Since I can't get it from you

You're always busy
You're always tired
You're overworked
You're underpaid
You got an attitude with me
'Cuz your baby daddy didn't come see you today

I am your son
I am your daughter
I am a priority
God gave you the authority

To provide for me
To protect me
To teach me about responsibility
To comfort me
To laugh with me
To discipline me

And to always be honest with me
So take the time to spend some time with me
I don't need you to be my friend
I need you to be my mama
I need you to be my daddy
I need you to help me
Become the best me I can be

SOMEBODY TOUCHED ME

Somebody touched me the wrong way
And nobody did anything about it
So I'll cry about it
I'll sing about it
I'll scream about it
I'll talk about it
I'll tell somebody about it

Somebody touched me the wrong way
My mama had a clue
My daddy never knew
I was only a child
A girl child
Somebody touched me in the secret place
And I didn't tell nobody but God

I don't bother nobody
I play with my Barbie dolls
Have tea parties
Make mud pies
Or I make sand castles in the sand

I dream of one day becoming a model
Or singing songs like Beyonce
I watch my favorite TV shows
I smile every time Sugar Mama chases Pappy
Or wonder what it's like to get premonitions
Like Raven

I just wanted to look in the mirror
And see the sun shine
Because I smiled today

Somebody touched me the wrong way
And I needed to say it
Because it hurts
And I wanted it to stop
And it will only stop if I make it stop

So today
I'll yell
I'll scream
I will let go of my fear
And say it
So that other girls
Won't let it happen to them

Somebody touched me the wrong way
Somebody touched me in the secret place
And it wasn't my fault
It was never my fault

I was just a child
Just a girl child
Looking in the mirror
Waiting for the sun to shine
Because I smiled today

Somebody touched me in the secret place
And I told you
And there will be no more silence
Because if somebody is touching you
You need to tell somebody too

A RAINY VALENTINE

It's raining outside
The clouds resemble
A white silvery blanket
No blue skies today
And the sun won't even shine

It's Valentines Day
And in my mind
I'm thinking happy love day
A smile comes across my face
As I think about
The man I love today

He is so beautiful
And even amidst the backdrop of dark clouds
I see the sun about to shine
As I think about this love of mine

In his presence
The essence of who he is
Causes my heart to sing new songs
Tonight
I'll light purple candles
As I wait for him to join me
I will present him with fragrant flowers
A sweet aroma for my love
I wait patiently for him

He has turned my dark days
Into rays of sunshine
He mended my broken heart
And with each new day
His love amazes me more and more

My dear Jesus
Your death on the cross
Has made me see
There is no greater love
Than the love between you and me

Happy Valentines Day my love
Because of you my life has changed
Because our love has eternal gain

WAITING ON BIG DADDY

I sat down and began to think about my love life
My thoughts carefully focused on the many failed
relationships
How each one had taken away a piece of me

I thought about the many sacrifices
To make each relationship work
What I gave up to be in love

What I gave up
Was more precious than the relationship itself
I gave up me
Giving up my wants and
My needs
My desires
Transforming into his ideal woman

Love is truly delicious
Holding hands and making love
Gentle touches and
Sweet kisses and
Stimulating conversations

I remember waiting for his call
Each time the phone rang
Holding my breath
As I waited
For the voice on the other end to speak

How are you baby
Slowly I began to exhale
His words reached out and touched me

I respond slowly
Hey baby
How are you

My day could have been hell
I could have been mad with the world
But when Big Daddy called
'Everythang was alright

Closing my eyes
I listened to the sound
The tone
Clinging to each word he said
Keeping my eyes closed
I tuned out everything around me
'Cause when Big Daddy spoke I listened

That's when I remembered
That's when it came to me
What a fool I've been
Sitting on the phone waiting for Big Daddy

I could have been a model
A movie star
Who knows I could have been a rocket scientist
But oh no
I've been spending my time on the phone
Waiting for Big Daddy to call

I'm not blaming anybody
I make my own choices in my life
So this poem is not about male bashing

I thought I couldn't live
Without Big Daddy
I thought I couldn't move without Big Daddy
I thought I couldn't sleep
Without Big Daddy laying by my side
The only thing I had time for
Was trying to figure out
How to see more of Big Daddy

I had to learn
That there was life beyond Big Daddy
That when Big Daddy left
He went on with his life
And I was left picking up the pieces to mine
My mama always said
A man can only do
What a woman allows

STRONG BLACK WOMAN

Dedicated to Danielle Simpson, A special ten-year old girl.
You are a leader. You are our future.

Like Harriet Tubman
I'm strong and black
Like Sojourner Truth
I'm a powerful black woman
Who calls on God
And my God
Answers me back

Like Fannie Lou Hamer
I will fight for what is right
Ain't no mountain too high
No river too wide
I'm on a mission
Making sure all of my people
Make it to freedom's side

I hold in my hands
The future of the world
The ancestors have given me a story to tell

God has empowered me
To tell his story
I'm a kingdom builder
So that God gets the glory

So now you know
Just who I am
I'm Danielle Simpson
A strong black woman
With a story to tell

TAKE ME BACK

Today I will turn off my TV
Every single day nothing but
Rape
Murder
Missing children
Pseudo terrorist attacks
And I don't know who has the most fame
R. Kelly
Or Osama Bin-Laden

I wanna go back
Back to the old days
When life was simple
And the world was a better place

I wanna go back to my turquoise
Banana seat bike with the white basket on the front
Please take me back to the days of
Double Dutch
Hopscotch
Old Maid, War, and Hide and go Seek

Take me back to a dime bag of chips
With hot sauce poured on top
Take me back to Blow Pops
Apple Now and Laters and Nut Chews

Take me back to quarter basement parties
With black lights
And sweaty black children
Dancing to the sounds of Earth Wind and Fire
Who had reasons
The Isley Brothers were in between the sheets

Marvin Gaye had the distant lover
And Al Green was looking for love and happiness
And let us never forget that the mother ship had landed
And we all did the Atomic Dog together

Take me back to fun times
Like Adventure Land
Riverview
And Fun Town

Take me back to a time
When black homes had a mama and a daddy
A time when we sat at the table
Said grace and ate together

Take me back to the days
When being gay
Meant you were happy

Take me back to Saturday mornings
With a bowl of Apple Jacks
Captain Crunch or Sugar Frosted Flakes
As you waited patiently for Mama to turn her back
And proceeded to pour the bowl of milk down the drain
'Cause all kids liked cereal but hated to drink the milk

Take me back to cartoons that were funny
Like the Jetsons, Tom and Jerry and who didn't like
Bugs Bunny or Ricochet Rabbit

Take me back to Sunday mornings
With Jubilee Showcase
With Mahalia Jackson, the Norfleet Brothers, Shirley
Ceaser and the Caravans
And believe me you were going to church

Whether you liked it or not

Please take me back when
Wearing an afro was symbolic of black pride
And we were a part of the nappy head revolution

Take me back to a time
When revolution was real
Family had foundation
And leadership was in all of us

Take me back to a time
When love was honorable
The black man was king
The black woman his queen
And we were the victors
And not the victims

Take me back
Please take me back

Thank You
for reading and supporting

Somebody Better Say Something

by

"Mama" Brenda Matthews

To order additional copies, contact us or invite "Mama" Brenda Matthews to your next literary/literacy event, book signing, conference, poetry reading, slam, open mic, K-12, charter, college, university, church, conference, expo, concert, corporation, community organization you may contact the publisher at:

Email: books@ebonyenergy.com

On-line Bookstore: www.ebonyenergybooks.com

Distributors: amazon.com, Baker & Taylor, Biblio

This book can be ordered anywhere in the world where books are sold and distributed by the ISBN:

ISBN: 1-59825-012-4   Retail Price: $19.95 USD*
*ISBN13: 978-1-59825-012-1
Volume/Trade/Special Discounts Available
Publisher prices may be higher in other countries.

EbonyEnergy Publishing, Inc. (NFP)
P.O. Box 43476 Chicago, IL 60643-0476
773-779-8129 (o) 773-779-8139 (f)
www.ebonyenergy.com

About The Author

"Mama" Brenda Matthews

Photo by Abena

Brenda Matthews, affectionately known as *Mama Brenda,* is a poet pregnant with purpose. That purpose is to plant seeds of change in the hearts of those who have fallen through the cracks. She has traveled throughout the United States and Africa to deliver her message of change to the *'least of these.'* Mama Brenda's poetry passion has been widely recognized. A two-time featured poet of HBO's Def Poetry Jam Chicago, she has shared the stage with The Last Poets, Vanessa Bell Armstrong, Malcolm Jamal Warner and Albertina Walker, to name a few. *Mama Brenda* has written and produced through her production company

Imani Nia two CDs entitled, "A Piece of My Soul" and "Tapestry of the Heart." Imani Nia through Taproots, Inc., a nonprofit organization, uses spoken word as a tool to teach life skills, alcohol, tobacco and HIV prevention in Chicago Public Schools. She has performed in the independent film *Love Your Mama* and in the 2001 production of Dance Africa Chicago.

"There is power in the spoken word. God created the universe with the spoken word. *In the beginning was the word... (Luke 1:1).* The spoken word can restore the black man, empower his seed and reconcile his family. I will continue to perform in prisons, drug rehabilitation centers, and shelters, to speak words that transform lives."

www.ingramcontent.com/pod-product-compliance
Lightning Source LLC
Chambersburg PA
CBHW021340090426
42742CB00008B/668